The Mirror

Brandon Robshaw

Published in association with
The Basic Skills Agency

Hodder & Stoughton

A MEMBER OF THE HODDER HEADLINE GROUP

Acknowledgements
Cover: Stuart Williams
Illustrations: Dave Smith

Orders: please contact Bookpoint Ltd, 78 Milton Park, Abingdon, Oxon OX14
4TD. Telephone: (44) 01235 827720, Fax: (44) 01235 400454. Lines are open
from 9.00–6.00, Monday to Saturday, with a 24 hour message answering service.
Email address: orders@bookpoint.co.uk

British Library Cataloguing in Publication Data
A catalogue record for this title is available from The British Library

ISBN 0 340 80056 9

First published 2001
Impression number   10 9 8 7 6 5 4 3 2 1
Year   2007 2006 2005 2004 2003 2002 2001

Copyright © 2001 Brandon Robshaw

Typeset by SX Composing DTP, Rayleigh, Essex.
Printed in Great Britain for Hodder & Stoughton Educational, a division of
Hodder Headline Plc, 338 Euston Road, London NW1 3BH by Athenaeum
Press, Gateshead, Tyne and Wear.

The Mirror

Contents

1

On Holiday

Louise was young, pretty and on holiday.
She sat outside a café in the south of France.

Louise put her hand to her head.
She had a headache.
She had been out with
her friends Sue and Isabel last night.
They'd overdone it a bit.
Drinking in one bar after another.

Sue and Isabel were still in bed at the hotel.
Louise had come out on her own.
She needed a bit of fresh air.
She sipped her coffee slowly.

These cafés were expensive.
She would have liked to sit here all day.
Waiting for her headache to go.
Maybe have a light lunch here.

But she couldn't do that.
She'd spent too much money last night.
It was a drag, not having enough money.
It meant you couldn't enjoy things properly.
She looked at the boats in the harbour.
Lucky people, thought Louise.
They had plenty of money.

A shadow fell across her table.
Louise looked up.
An old man was standing there.
His hair was white. He was leaning on a stick.

'Excuse me, my dear,' he said.
'Do you mind if I join you?'

2

Champagne

Louise looked round the café.
Other tables were free.
Why didn't the old man sit at one of them?
Still, she didn't want to be rude.
'Sure,' she said. 'Sit down.'

The old man sat down, slowly and stiffly.
He was wearing a smart suit and a gold watch.
He looked like a rich man.
'Lovely day,' he said.
'My name's Charles Maltby, by the way.'

He smiled and put out his thin, bony hand.
Louise shook it. 'Hi. I'm Louise.'

'A very pretty name,' said Charles.
'Waiter! Could we have a bottle of champagne
at this table, please? And two glasses!'
he called out.

'Not for me, thanks,' said Louise.
'I'm just having a coffee.
Then I'm meeting my friends.'

'I am so sorry,' said Charles.
'I should have asked you first.'

He sounded so polite that
Louise couldn't be angry.
'It's all right,' she said.

'Now I shall have to drink
all the champagne myself!'
said the old man.
'Are you on holiday here?
And who are your friends?'

So Louise told him
all about Sue and Isabel.
About how they shared a flat together.
How they'd all come on holiday
for two weeks to get away
from their boring jobs.

The old man was a good listener.
He nodded his head.
He asked questions.
He really was a nice old man,
thought Louise.
Probably a bit lonely.

The champagne arrived.
Charles poured himself a glass.
Then he looked at Louise.
'Are you sure you won't . . .?'

The champagne did look nice.
'All right, then, thanks,' said Louise.

The champagne made Louise talk more.
Charles kept filling her glass.
She told him all about her job in the office.
How she hated it.
How she wished she had more money.

'Ah, but you are young,' said Charles.
'That's what counts.
Look at me – I have more money
than I know what to do with.
But I'm an old man.'

'You're not that old,' said Louise.
It wasn't true,
but she wanted to please him.

Charles smiled. 'Thank you.'
'Would you like to have dinner
with me tonight?'

'Dinner?' said Louise.
'Well, I don't know . . .'
'On my yacht,' said Charles.
'That one there.'
He pointed at the biggest,
most beautiful yacht
in the harbour.

3

Dinner on the Yacht

Louise's friends couldn't believe it
when she told them.
'You met a man and he asked you to dinner
on his yacht!' said Sue.
'Some people have all the luck!'

'How old is he?' asked Isabel.

'Well, he's quite old,' said Louise.
'He looks about eighty.'

'You can't go on a dinner date
with a man of eighty!' said Sue.
'He's old enough to be your grandfather!'

'I don't care,' said Louise.
'He's nice and he's very rich.'

That night, Louise put on her short white dress.
'She's wearing her pulling dress!' said Sue.
Louise ignored her.

A tall man in a suit stood waiting by the yacht.
'I'm Karl,' he said. 'Mr Maltby's servant.'

He led Louise up the steps.
Charles Maltby was sitting in a chair on deck.
He was wearing a dinner jacket and a bow tie.
He got up slowly, using his stick.
'How lovely to see you, my dear!'
He kissed her on both cheeks.
'Let's go to the dining cabin
and have a glass of wine.'

The dining cabin had wooden walls
and fur rugs on the floor.
It was dark and cosy.
Candles were flickering.
There was a big oval mirror on the wall.
It had a gold frame.
The candles made little gold points of light in it.
Louise caught a glimpse of herself
in the mirror.
'What a beautiful mirror!' she said.

'Yes, it's a magic mirror!' said Charles.
'Mirror, mirror, on the wall,
who is the fairest of them all?
Louise, of course!'

Louise looked at herself in the mirror.
She did look pretty good.
Charles came and stood behind her.
He put his hand on her shoulder.
They looked good together, thought Louise.
The young woman in white
and the old man in black.
It was like a picture.

'May I ask you a question?' said Charles.

'Of course,' said Louise.

'I know we've only just met
but . . . will you marry me?'

4

Marriage

Louise's friends couldn't believe it
when she told them.
'You're going to marry him?' said Sue.
'You must be mad!' said Isabel.
'He's sixty years older than you!' said Sue.
'And you've only just met him!' said Isabel.

'I don't care,' said Louise.
'He's really nice. And he's really rich.'

'You're just marrying him for his money!'
said Sue.

'Let's face it,' said Louise.
'He's not going to live forever.
I can cheer up the last few years of his life.
When he dies, I get all his money.
Nobody loses out. What's the problem?'

'Don't do it, Louise,' said Isabel.

'I've made up my mind,' said Louise.
'I'm going to marry him.'

Charles and Louise were married
a month later, in London.

5

A Wedding Present

Charles had a huge house in London.
It was like a castle.
Louise had to pinch herself
to make sure she wasn't dreaming.

'I've got a present for you, my dear,'
said Charles.
'My beautiful magic mirror –
the one you saw on the yacht – it's yours now.'

The big oval mirror hung on the wall
of Louise's bedroom.
'A beautiful woman needs a beautiful mirror,'
said Charles.
'Just promise me you'll look in it every day.
That's very important.'

'I will,' said Louise. 'And thank you!'
She looked at herself in the mirror.
She looked older, somehow,
now she was married.

The weeks went by quickly.
Louise gave up her office job, of course.
She didn't have to do any housework.
Karl did all that.

She went shopping.
She took up riding.
Every day, she looked in her mirror
and thought how lucky she was.

The mirror showed a happy face
looking back at her.
But she was starting to look older.
Every day she looked, there were more lines
on her face.
Round her mouth
and at the corners of her eyes.

By the time autumn came,
her hair was starting to go grey.

6

Sue and Isabel Visit

Louise looked in her mirror.
She didn't like what she saw.
Every day, when she looked in the mirror,
her face was a little bit older.

Sue and Isabel were coming for lunch today.
Louise wished they weren't coming.
She didn't want to be seen like this.

There was a knock at the door.
Karl let Sue and Isabel in.

'Hi, Sue! Hi, Isabel!'
said Louise, trying to sound happy.

Sue and Isabel stared at her.
'Louise! What the hell's happened to you?'
said Sue.

'What do you mean?'

'You know – the grey hair and that,'
said Isabel.
'You look so much older.'

'Rubbish!' said Louise, trying to laugh.
'Just a touch of grey, that's all.'

'You don't look well, Louise,' said Sue.

'I'm very well, thank you,' said Louise.
She felt angry with Sue.
'I'm very happy, all right?'

'How's Charles?' asked Isabel,
changing the subject.
'Is he here?'

'He's very well too,' said Louise.
'He's not here. He's out running.'

'Running!' said Sue.
'At his age! I don't believe it!'

'He's very fit for his age,' said Louise.
'He seems to get fitter every day.'

Marriage seemed to suit Charles.
He seemed to be getting younger.

'Let me show you round the house,'
said Louise.
At least they'd be impressed with the house.

They were.
'What a beautiful room!' said Isabel,
when she saw Louise's pink bedroom.
'I don't like the mirror, though,' said Sue.

'It was a present from Charles,' said Louise.
'Why don't you like it?'

'I don't know.
It just gives me the creeps.'

The remark annoyed Louise.
She wouldn't ask Sue and Isabel round again.

7

Grey Hair

Every day, the mirror showed Louise
an older face.
It was frightening.
But she couldn't stop looking in the mirror.
Looking for new signs of age.

Her hair was nearly all grey now.
'I look terrible, don't I?'
she said to Charles.

Charles kissed her.
'Nonsense, my dear. You look lovely.'

Charles was looking younger all the time.
He didn't use his stick any more.
His hair wasn't white any more.
It was a dark grey now.

'Maybe I should borrow
some of your hair dye!' said Louise.

'What do you mean?
I don't use hair dye, my dear.'

'But – when I met you –
your hair was white!'

'You are mistaken, my dear.
My hair has never been white.'
He came and stood behind Louise.
He put his hand on her shoulder.
'Don't we look a charming couple?'
said Charles.

Louise stared in the mirror.
It must have been a trick of the light.
But she and Charles looked the same age now.

8

Winter

Winter came.
Louise started to get aches and pains.
She had to give up her riding.

Sometimes she felt as if the mirror
was draining the life out of her.
But she couldn't stop looking in it.
She watched her hair get whiter and whiter.
One day, as she was brushing it,
her hair started to come out.
Great clumps of it.

Louise started to cry.
'What's happening to me?
I'm falling to pieces!'

Charles came into the room.
He moved very lightly and swiftly now.
'Nonsense, my dear.
There is nothing to worry about.'
He kissed her softly on the cheek.
As if he was kissing an old lady.

The next morning,
something horrible happened.
Louise was cleaning her teeth.
There was a sudden clatter.
Then another, and another.
Her teeth were falling out
into the washbasin.

'Never mind, my dear,'
said Charles.
'We'll get you a new set.
The best that money can buy!'

9

The Dentist

'Open wide,' said the dentist.
'Yes, they'll all have to come out.
We'll make you up a new set.
You've done well to keep your teeth so long.
At your age . . .'

'What do you mean, at my age?' said Louise.
'I'm twenty-one!'

The dentist looked at her strangely.
He didn't say anything.

Louise went home in a taxi.
Tears rolled down her cheeks.
What had happened to her?

She let herself into the house.
Charles was standing in the hall.
He was wearing a white suit.
His hair was black.
He looked very tall and straight.

'What – what's happened here?'
said Louise. 'What's going on?'
She took a few steps towards him.
She stumbled and fell to the ground.

Charles picked her up in his strong arms.
He carried her upstairs.

He sat her on the bed in front of the mirror.
Louise saw herself,
a little old woman dressed in black.
Behind her stood Charles –
a tall, strong young man in a white suit.

'It's that mirror, isn't it?' said Louise suddenly.
Her voice sounded weak and old.
'It's drained my life away. Taken my youth.'

Charles laughed. 'Nonsense, my dear.'

Louise picked up a heavy, metal hairbrush.
She raised her arm.
'I'm going to smash that mirror!'

10

Death

'Oh no,' said Charles.
'You mustn't smash my magic mirror.
That's what keeps me young.'
He plucked the hairbrush from Louise's hand.

Louise felt funny.
There was a kind of bang in her brain.
In the mirror, she saw that
she was falling sideways.
She hit the ground.
Everything went dark.

She heard the ambulance arrive.
She wanted to tell someone about the mirror.
But she couldn't speak.
The ambulance set off, siren going.
Too loud, thought Louise.
It was the last thing she thought.
She was dead on arrival.

The doctor said a stroke was the cause of death.
But really that was just what finished her off.
The main cause of death was simply old age.

After the funeral,
Charles Maltby stood looking in the mirror.
He saw a tall, handsome young man.
About twenty years old. He smiled.

'I'm tired of this cold weather, Karl,' he said.
'I want to go somewhere hot.
Go and pack, would you?'

'Yes, sir,' said Karl.
'Will you be taking the mirror?'

'Oh no,' said Charles.
'I won't be needing that for a few years.'